THE WARRIORS OF WRIDOR

The Doomed Quest

KAUTILYA JAMMALAMADAKA

The Warriors of Wridor is a work of fiction. Names, characters, places and incidents are the products of author's imagination or are used fictitiously. Any resemblance to actual events, locales, or persons, living or dead, is entirely coincidental.

Summary: After going to the alternative world of earth, Jack Wridor soon finds himself in a whirlpool of danger.

Prologue

If you are reading this, you are probably reading this for a reason. Just keep in mind that this is real. This may include some truths you might not want to know. If you want to stay innocent and not know about these horrors, you are better off not reading this. However, if you want to know the truth, you should read this. This will change your life forever. You soon will meet the Warriors of Wridor. Soon, you will be surrounded by danger. You have been warned ☺

Have fun,

Kautilya J

For my beloved teacher Mrs. Kellogg

A Strange Visitor

The last thing that wasn't on Jack's summer to do list was to get attacked by a monster. Correction: lots of monsters. He wished to have a normal summer without any unusual things happening. But a monster- free summer was not what was heading his way, just the opposite.

The whole mess started when a girl from the magical world decided to pay Jack a visit. As soon as he got to the abandoned train track, the hope to have a normal summer started to crumble.

It all began on one Friday, the last day of school. For most people, summer meant three months of fun, but for Jack it was the start of three months of danger, crazy stuff, and tons of near death experiences. Since then, the hope for having a fun summer went out of the window. For the most part, Jack was running for his life. That's when he got sick of summer.

It started in the morning when Jack was combing his thick, curly and crazy brown hair.

His reflection stared at him. For an eleven year old boy, his face was weary. His brown eyes had an intense seriousness that matched his penetrating personality. He looked as if he had never smiled in his life.

Jack was combing his hair, but his thoughts were elsewhere. They were straying to summer break. He wondered if something exciting would happen.

He had no answer, and his hair was still insanely curly. He gave up like always and started walking towards the kitchen. He barreled into his dad as he was looking for his cereal. "I've been looking for you," his dad said.

Jack's dad was looking at him curiously and said "someone is at the door for you", in his deep voice and continued "Long Dark Hair, pretty face, icy blue eyes."

Jack was perplexed. *"I don't have any friend like that,"* he thought. But curious, he opened the door. The next thing he knew, Jack was grabbed and thrown onto the street. He fell, his body aching. Jack stood up groaning and gasping.

That's when he got his first look at the girl. Sure, he was popular, he has seen pretty girls before but this girl was totally... wow. She had dark hair, a pretty face, and icy eyes that seemed to see through Jack. But what really caught Jack's attention were her clothes. She wore a black leather jacket, ripped blue jeans, black leather boots and a white t-shirt. It was just a basic punk vibe.

Jack opened his mouth to speak, but he was cut short. "Jack Wridor" she said sharply. "Get your friend Luke and follow me to the abandoned train track."

"Whoa, whoa, whoa," Jack said. "You throw me across the street and then tell me to follow you to the abandoned train track? I'm not allowed to go there, but you are? You don't look older than eleven. Even the adults avoid it, but you can go there when you want?" Jack challenged.

The girl didn't flinch. "I know the rumors about the train track, thank you very much, but I told you to follow me. If you don't come, I'll take your friend alone." Jack gulped. "Fine," he muttered. He regretted it as soon as it came out of his mouth.

As soon as Luke saw the girl, his mouth fell open in awe. Luke, having brown hair that stuck out around his round babyish face, and mischievous little eyes, he didn't look very charming. So he was glad to be walking with a pretty girl and didn't care where and why.

Jack, on the other hand, was very nervous and gnawed on his fingernails. He didn't want to go, but curiosity got the better of him.

The trio kept on walking until they reached the rusty train track.

The girl stopped suddenly, making Jack and Luke nearly knock into her. She turned and gave them an icy look. She then raised her arms into an arc. Lights flashed. Then everything blacked out.

When Jack woke up, he was in a different place. The abandoned train track was nowhere in sight, but that was impossible unless they had been knocked out and sent to the other side of the country. It did look very desolate, as there were no buildings and no sign of life. There were no trees, grass or any kind of nature. The land held nothing but sand... and danger. Or rather, dangers held the land.

"Creepy" was the word that came to Jack's mind. The desolated plot of land gave a dark vibe that said *"Stay away or else..."*

Luke was totally losing his mind. Sure, the girl had been pretty and all, but the thought that he was being kidnapped by a witch in punk clothes was weird, very weird. The whole idea of getting kidnapped was creepy enough. The thought of magic just gave him the creeps.

"*Stay away or else...*" This time, it wasn't a vibe. It was a voice. Then, the ground cracked. A fearsome creature came into sight. It turned towards Jack.

A Near Death Experience

The monster was seven feet tall. Its whole body was… green. Its torso was bare, exposing a six-pack. Its legs were stout and short, but Jack had a feeling that the monster could outrun him if it wanted. Its arms were built with powerful muscle, as if the monster worked out for years with the one purpose of beating Jack silly. It's face... totally weird. It looked like a saber toothed tigers face, but it was covered in scales.

Its eyes were completely orange. But the weirdest part was the teeth. Instead of the famous curved saber-teeth, they were triangular and had dried blood on them…, totally disgusting. It snarled, making his face even uglier.

"I have been waiting for you, Jack Wridor". Jack's mind was blank. Jack's first thought was *"Did I meet this guy before? Probably not."* All Jack knew was that he was famous. OR WAS HE INFAMOUS? To a monster, probably number two.

The Monster growled and charged. Its leg lashed out and connected with Jack's chest. Jack staggered. The monster laughed as he watched Jack double over in pain. "Is that all you have? Everyone has compared you to the greatest hero. Is this all you got? Come on, Wridor. Kill me." The monster roared in laughter.

"Think," Jack thought. *"What do I have? My books? No. My phone? No. I have nothing that would kill him."* The realization dawned on him, to the fright that he would be beaten up and the relief that he wouldn't need to fight.

He looked at the monster. "Heroes are proud in victory, and humble in defeat. I cannot beat you. That is the truth."

"Noble words," the monster said. "But not quite right. Heroes are able to fight obstacles. You aren't. You are no hero. For one that many have praised of, you are weak. You don't deserve to live."

The monster charged.

This time, Jack was ready. He sidestepped the monster's attack and added a solid blow of his own. The monster turned, only to get a fist in his face.

"So," Jack said. "I'm weak. What else? I'm also a martial artist."

The girl was watching all of this from a distance. "Stop," she commanded. "Wridor, you're enraging the monster. Impressive, though. You've got nobility and guts. If only you had strength, you would be a very formidable opponent." She turned towards the monster. "The test is over. Jack Wridor had shown his strengths. You are dismissed."

The monster turned. A moment later, he was gone.

Jack looked towards the girl. "So you mean that you sent this freaking monster after me to test my strengths?" He was steamed.

"Who gave you the right to test people anyway? Some lunatic who wants to train kids to become heroes? Where did you get the monster costume? Why did you get the monster costume? To scare people out of their wits?"

The girl smiled. "You'll find out. Don't worry. You're not being kidnapped. Taken from your home, maybe. But not kidnapped. I just don't want you to jump out of the car when I'm driving.

Luke stared. "You can drive?"

The girl nodded.

"Look," Jack said. "Whoever you are, this joke is sick. It didn't fool me. If you can drive," Jack said. Where's your car?"

"Oh, I was hoping you would ask," the girl said. "Follow me. I'll show you."

Soon, Jack, Luke and the mysterious girl were rumbling along dirt roads in a blue pick-up truck. The girl was driving pedal to the metal, her speed never dropping less than hundred miles per hour. Luke was sitting in the passenger seat, examining the girl from every angle. Jack sat on the pick-up bed alone, replaying the day. The Monster who attacked them, the strange witch princess who took them from home, and the car in the middle of nowhere. Was that all a sick joke?

Jack was so intent in his thoughts, he didn't notice anything until Luke screamed. "Are you crazy?" He yelled at the girl. You're headed right for the river!"

Jack's head snapped up. He craned his neck to see. Sure enough, there was a river. And they were headed right for it.

Jack's first thought was, "*I don't know how to swim.*" His panic radar went up. He tried to brace himself for the impact. He wanted to yell, but his voice wasn't working. His breath came out in wheezes.

Luke was thinking, *"should I jump over the side of pick-up truck, No, it is going too fast."*

Jack closed his eyes and waited for him to drown. But, it didn't come.

Marble columns shot up from underneath the river. With it came billowing mist.

A crescendo of voices accompanied it. "State your business."

The girl looked up. "I have come with trainees. Let me in. The password is arona.

The billowing smoke started moving towards them. Then, it swallowed them whole.

Galobia

The thing that surprised Luke was that they had landed in a room. There were already hundred weird things that happened today, but still. And as an added bonus, the room had to be breathtaking.

The room's walls were made out of marble. They were adored with carvings of war chariots and strange objects that looked like weapons. Life size statues of muscular men were displayed in the four corners of the room. Their hands were raised towards the mahogany ceiling, where the candles from a diamond chandelier cast a soft light over the room.

There were many displays on the walls such as oil paintings and war banners. They all had captions underneath them, telling the story of each. Some were dramatic, and others were not. But the most interesting thing was in the middle of the room, placed on a small table. It was a model country. But the thing that was so interesting was the fact that the model country seemed alive. As Jack studied the country closely, he noticed that the country looked like a lot of beautiful landscapes and villages in one place. The north was a lush green forest, and at its edge there were a few cottages with smoke coming out of their chimneys. The east was a prairie, and in the west were green grassy hills. The south was crowded with snowcapped mountains. They raised high above the other landscapes. The most spectacular sight was in the center of the country. It was a city. A white castle rose in the center, set on a mountain.

The castle shared the hill with four watch towers, four walls and a moat. Instead of crocodiles in the moat, there were five old fashioned ships with cannons perched on the deck. Jack glanced back at the girl. She was leaning casually on one of the walls. "So," she said. "If you are done admiring Thekerion's models, I better introduce you to him." She opened a door next to her.

"Is Thekerion a dangerous Wizard?" Jack asked, his voice dripping with sarcasm.

The girl shrugged," I guess, kind of". Jack smiled and held the door open. "Ladies first."

Luke was wondering whether this was just some kind of joke, but the person at the other end of the corridor was too real to be part of a joke.

Reclining on a golden throne was a middle aged man with slightly wrinkled brown skin and heavy brows.

Luke frowned. "You know, for a wizard, you look downright normal." The man didn't smile "Wizards are not as you think, boy. Lead this one to his building and assist him," he told the girl. He then pointed to Jack. "I need to talk to this young man."

The girl nodded and led Luke through the doorway.

"You," Thekerion began when they were alone. "You know my name is Jack," Jack blurted out. Thekerion paid no heed. "In this city," he said," I tell people what to do and they do it".

Jack rolled his eyes. Thekerion said "and I ask you to go on an expedition." That caught Jack unaware. "Um, no. I don't think so."

"Do you want to go to Jail," Thekerion said sharply. It wasn't a question. Jack shifted uncomfortably in his chair.

Thekerion took that as "No".

"Great" Thekerion replied," you will find weapons in your building. The expedition will start tomorrow. Read your book and I will lead you to your building.

"Wait a minute," Jack said. "What expedition is it? Who's going with me?"

Thekerion held his hands up. "The expedition is to find the location of the enemy. He is a traitor. Up in the north, there's an inn called the One Inn. In it is a man named Count Derin. He will give you information.

After getting the information, come back and give me your report. And you will have two companions. Emmera, the girl who took you here and a boy named L.J. And by the way, don't forget to read the book. You want to know about our history, you have to read it. It will be in your building. Your building will also have weapons, clothes, etc."

"Whoa, wait up," Jack said. "I don't know where my building is. I don't know where the One Inn is, and I don't know how to use a weapon. If you want a fierce warrior to go on an expedition and report enemy locations, you have the wrong guy. I've never picked up a weapon in my life, much less used one. You want a warrior. I'm not a warrior. I'm a kid. Whose stupid idea was it anyway to take kids and make them go on expeditions? I refuse."

Thekorion didn't flinch. "I see your problem. But let me repeat what I said. You either go on the expedition or you go to jail. I've never seen anybody prefer jail. Why? It's not fun, let me tell you. Lots of torture. I'd never want something like torture to happen to you."

Something in Thekerion's voice made Jack think that he didn't care whatsoever.

"You'll go on the expedition," Thekorion said, this time more forcefully. "I'll introduce you to L.J. and lead you to your building." Thekorion held his hand out to Jack. "Let's shake. The expedition is nothing personal. So, let's shake. It's a formality that you are used to, I'm sure."

"Actually," Jack said. "It's not a formality on earth to shake hands with someone who makes you do something against their will. We call them tyrants, and we put *them* in jail. If anybody deserves to be in jail, it's you."

Thekorion stiffened. His muscles tightened, and his fists clenched. Jack could almost hear him counting to ten. Finally, his muscles loosened and he smiled. It did not reach his eyes, not even for one second.

"Well," he said, clearing his throat. "I'll lead you to your building. You need to be there. *Now.*"

Luke found the buildings more impressive than the people. Sure, they were warriors in training, blah, blah, blah. **But so what?** The architecture was amazing. *"Better than the roman standards, even,"* Luke thought. The castle looming on the small cottages and large manors alike, the clean cobblestone streets that were loud yet peaceful and the bustling city that was organized A to Z. It all seemed like paradise to Luke.

"Hey, watch it!"

Luke looked away from the buildings. Standing in front of him was a large girl. His foot had stubbed her toe.

"I-I'm sorry," he stuttered. I just was-"

"Looking at the architecture?" The girl asked.

Luke nodded.

"Well, I don't blame you for stubbing my toe." She studied Luke. "You're new, right?"

"Yeah. I'm Luke." He held out his hand.

The girl took it. "I'm Katie. It was nice to meet you."

When Jack walked with Thekorion, people of all ages turned to stare. While they stared, Jack was all eyes for the city. "The model of Galobia is a replica of the real city," Thekorion said. "Except the fact that the real city is much bigger and has more stuff, the model is accurate."

Thekorion was right. There were many training grounds in the city that were not included in the model city. Children, teens and adults all were training furiously. There were many weapons. Swords to spears to maces, they were all there.

"Hey L.J.," Thekorion called to a tall boy at a training arena. "I've found a third member for your expedition."

That got the boy's attention. He dropped his sword and ambled over. "L.J., meet Jack. He is quiet temperamental. Jack, meet L.J. Scout, soldier, you name it."

The boys sized each other up. L.J. stood a full head taller and was more muscular.

"Well, hello Jack. I'm glad you are with us. See you tomorrow. We'll meet you at the outskirts of Galobia." Jack nodded.

L.J. turned and walked away. "Big guy," Jack observed.

"Big guy, small brain," a voice said from behind him.

Jack turned. Standing behind him was a burly redhead. His brown eyes lingered on Jack. "My name is Jared. So you're a new trainee, huh," he said. "When I was a trainee, I had to do an expedition. I spent a week in the enemy's army as a spy. So, what are you doing?"

"I have to get information out of Count Derin," Jack replied. "Whoever he is."

"You've got to get information out of Count Derin? I feel sorry for you. He is a tough nut."

"He is?" Jack gulped.

Thekorion cleared his throat. "So Jack, your building is over there. He pointed towards a cabin on a hill.

"You have to climb, of course," Thekorion said.

Jack looked up. "Great."

Whatever Jack expected the cabin to be was wrong. For one thing, it smelled like cat litter. For another, it looked like a torture house. Cobwebs hung from the walls, and the floorboards creaked when Jack moved. The walls were plastered with old photographs. The bed was sodden with water, and the ceiling was rotting. The only thing that looked new in the room was a wooden drawer.

"Some cabin," Jack muttered. Just then, his phone buzzed. Jack took it out. His dad had texted him.

Where r u?

I've been looking for u.

R u ok?

Jack sighed. What could he say? *"Oh, dad, I forgot to tell you that I got into this magical world where I have to go on an expedition to drill information out of this Count. You don't mind, do you?"* He didn't think so. If he did that, he would be dragged to a hospital for delusional people where nobody would even listen to him, much less believe him. Then again, Jack didn't completely believe it himself. He half expected himself to wake up. But he couldn't really prove that he was sleeping or that he was awake. *"People pinch themselves to make sure they are not dreaming, but how could anybody pinch themselves if they are asleep?"*

Jack shrugged. He stood up and walked towards the wooden drawer and opened it. The first cabinet was filled with stacks of camouflage clothes. "You've got to be kidding me," Jack said. "How can someone live on camouflage clothes? It seems horrible to wear nothing but camouflage. I'm keeping my clothes, even if they stink." He closed the cabinet and opened the next one. This one was even worse than the first. "Oh No." He said. "Healthy foods? Bags of peas, bread and nuts? Even the healthy school lunch program was better than this."

"Tell me about it," a voice said from behind him.

Standing outside the cabin was Luke. "How about letting me in," he called.

"I don't think you would like the smell of cat litter," Jack called back. Luke shrugged.

"Fine," Jack sighed and opened the door. Luke stepped in and took a breath. "Your cabin is better than mine. Mine smells like stale sweat and tobacco." Luke plopped himself onto the bed. "I have to ask you something," he said nervously.

"What?"

"Well, I'm afraid that this is all a dream. Do you really believe that we are here?"

Jack thought for a minute. Did *he* really believe that this was real?

"Yes, I do," he said. He wasn't so sure.

"Oh," Luke said, sounding relieved. "I just needed some assurance. I need to go now."

"Wait," Jack said. "Did you check out the bottom two drawers?"

Luke nodded.

"What's inside them then?"

"Well, in the third one, there are weapons. And," Luke added in a small voice. "I tried to use one."

Jack snorted. "Luke Smith using a weapon? That's the most hilarious thing I have ever heard."

Luke went pink.

"Sorry," Jack muttered. "What's in the fourth one?"

"A book," Luke said. "It's a book telling about this world."

Jack sucked in a breath. "A book about this world?"

Luke nodded. "It's actually kind of silly. The kind of the thing you would find in fairy tales."

Jack smiled. "Dude, I would read a girl's magazine to find out what's going on. I'm going to read."

Jack opened the book and began to read.

This was how the book began..........................

WELCOME TO OUR WORLD.

ONCE, THE WORLD PROSPERED. IT WAS GOVERNED BY TWO GODS. ONE GOVERNED GOODNESS, WHILE THE OTHER GOVERNED EVIL. AS DIFFERENT AS THEY WERE, THEY GOVERNED THE WORLD IN HARMONY.

THAT ALL CHANGED BECAUSE OF THE THREE. THEY WERE THE THREE FIRST PEOPLE ON THIS WORLD. AND THEY WERE EVIL. THEY WERE THE GREAT SORCERER WITH HIS MAGICAL SABER AND ARMY OF SORCERERS, SHAH ADDARE WITH HIS STAFF AND DEMON ARMY, AND VAROLON WITH HIS BOW AND HIS KNIGHTS.

THE THREE WEAPONS WERE THE FIRST OF THIS WORLD, AND THE MOST POWERFUL. THEY CONVINCED THE GOD OF EVIL TO WAGE WAR ON GOODNESS. THEIR PLAN WAS TO PUT EARTH TO ITS KNEES. THEREFORE, THE WARRIORS OF GOODNESS WENT TO YOUR WORLD. THEY WERE WARRIORS WHO KEPT PEACE IN GALOBIA AND OTHER PLACES.

BUT THE ATTACK NEVER CAME. NOBODY KNOWS WHY. THE THREE ARE STILL HERE, BUT THE GOD OF EVIL HAS NOT BEEN SEEN FOR FIVE BILLION YEARS.

AFTER EVERYTHING SETTLED DOWN, MANY OF THE WARRIORS SETTLED IN YOUR WORLD. THEIR BLOOD IS IN YOUR VEINS. NOW IN TIMES OF CRISIS, WE BRING YOU TO OUR WORLD. YOU ARE SUPPOSED TO BE IN OUR WORLD. THAT'S WHY YOU CAN GET HERE.

Jack frowned. He still didn't know who Count Derin is. He would just have to find out for himself.

Weapons lay on the floor. Jack studied the weapons closely. "No," he said, throwing aside a dagger. "Aha," he scooped a sword off the ground. "This looks good."

He slung the sword on his belt. "Cool," he said. "Even though I cannot use the sword, it'll make a good impression. I just need to figure out how to use one. I guess it won't take long."

He then walked down to meet Emmera and L.J.

Jack found Emmera and L.J. waiting for him in the out skirts of town, on a stretch of land that met the ocean. The sky was a bright orange as the sun rose.

Jack made his way up the rocks.

Emmera waved a greeting. "L.J. will scout ahead. We know that Count Derin should be staying at the One Inn. But he may not be there. If L.J. doesn't send a message, it means that Derin is still there."

"Or that I am captured" L.J. added. Emmera glared at him. You will visit the One Inn", she told Jack. "We can walk to there. The plan is to sneak up on Derin and beat him up. Then we tie him and force him to tell us what we need to know." She looked at Jack. "You can beat Derin up."

The Inn loomed ahead. Iron gates surrounded the building. The building itself was huge. It sat in the shade of oak trees, casting eerie shadows that sent a chill through Jack. Although it was noon, the building was dark.

"Okay,"Emmera said" I will go first and pretend to be a princess. I'll pay for a room, just so it wouldn't rouse suspicion. You attack later" Jack gulped. Emmera tossed over her shoulder, "Derin's room is the first one to the right on the second floor. Mine is the first one to the left on the third floor. Jack nodded. "I get it," he said. He didn't get it.

Jack pushed the Inn's doors open quietly. He stepped inside quickly and hurried towards the stairs. He could almost hear his own heart as he climbed up the stairs, hoping not to be seen.

"The first one to the right," Emmera had said.

Jack sucked in his breath and walked towards the door. His legs felt like lead as he walked towards the room on the far right. His hands trembled as he put them on the doorknob. His heart pounding, he wrenched the door open.

There was no one inside. The room was empty, literally. Not one thing was inside. Count Derin had left.

Jack turned to leave when he heard a voice behind him.

"Hey kid," said a voice from behind him.

"What are you doing?"

Jack's chest tightened. His breathing got fast and came out in wheezes. His heart filled with dread. He turned and came face to face with a tall armored man. He was armed with a sword.

"So you're Jack." The man's eyes inspected Jack. "You look very puny."

"Look," Jack said. "I'm looking for a man named Count Derin. He's an, uh, acquaintance of mine. You somehow know who I am, so you must know where he is. Can you point me towards him?"

The man's face spread into a leer. "You see, boy, I am Count Derin. And since you disturbed me, you will be punished severely."

"Lo-Look," Jack stuttered. "I just want information on the enemy. I can pay."

The man chuckled. "If I needed money, I could have destroyed this whole town. But that's not what I want. I am here on the behalf of Addare. I am here to rip you apart."

"I can give you a deal," Jack said. "If Addare sent you to rip me apart, you must be very formidable. That way, if you fight me, I would most likely lose. That's why I'm giving you a bet. If I win, you give me information. If you win, you'll kill me and have followed orders. It'll be a compromise." Jack felt stupid when he talked about compromises. If school bullies didn't care about compromises, why would a killer listen?

The Count's leer stretched even further. "If Addare ordered me to kill you, how do you think that you can stop me? I am not going to take the bet. I never take bets."

Jack was getting annoyed. "Dude, if you want to attack me, go ahead." He raised his sword. "I'm ready."

"I will attack. I will attack indeed. And I'm warning you; you will be dead."

The Count drew his sword and charged.

Arrows and Swords

Their swords met, again and again.
Silent but intimidating, The Count swung,
thrust, and parried with a silent force. The
Count parried Jack's thrust countered every
swing, intimidating Jack slowly but surely.

Every thrust was a force and every
swing an art. Jack was tiring under the perfect
attacks, his arms getting heavier, his strikes
slower and his confidence wavering. Count
Derin, sensing the weakness of Jack, pressed
forward. Switching gears, he pressed Jack back
with the ferocious swinging of a warrior,
surprisingly not leaving an inch of skin
exposed to the attacks. The Count pressed Jack
back. Their swords clashed only twice after
that. On the third swing, The Count deflected
the blade, kicked Jack back and knocked the
sword out of his hands, all of this in a few
seconds. He then launched himself onto Jack,
pummeling him with his hands.

Because of The Count's strength and weight advantage, he had Jack pinned to the ground in no time. Jack was struggling not to pass out. Jack's arms were pinned down, his legs were sore, and his attitude beat up. Jack only had one hope left, and it was Emmera. If anybody could show this dude, it was her. 'But she was too far away to signal to.' Or was she ....?

Luke held the bow in his left hand, the arrow knocked in his right hand. His target was a tree about 20 feet away. He was aiming for a hole about half way up the length of the tree. He peered from behind the bow, took a deep breath and let go. The arrow flew, looking as if it would hit its mark, until the last moment, when a draft of wind carried it into the air and made it land about 10 feet away." Not bad" said a voice from behind him. "We need to talk"

"I give up" Jack yelled. "Just let me tell you about the fair maiden who travels with me. I am her guard, as she was important to our quest. We were going to give her as a tribute. So, we were traveling. We ended up here. Not to draw attention she checked in first, and I was planning to be checked in few hours after her." Jack said "If I give her to you, will you let me go?" Derin raised his eyebrow." As I recall, I have heard of fair maiden. Bring her to me. I will either take her as a trainee or sell her as slave. Where is she?"

"Follow me," Jack said. "You lead the way. You will have to protect me from my enemies."

Derin nodded. "You have to pick up your sword though. You have to protect yourself too."

Jack nodded. Things could have not been more perfect.

After leading The Count up the long stone staircase, walking through the hallway, they finally reached Emmera's room. Jack gulped and opened the door, hoping that Emmera was ready to fight.

* * * * *

Katie stood behind Luke. She was wearing battle armor. She was carrying a spear in one hand and a shield in other.

"We need to talk," she repeated. I heard about the expedition and all, but the crucial fact is that many people, if not everybody except me, do not know this." She paused, waiting for Luke to react, when he didn't respond she continued. "The expeditions are a ploy. Thekerian sent Jack because evil forces need him to back them."

* * * * *

Emmera was nowhere to be seen. Though the room was clean and there are no signs of struggle, Jack knew that Emmera just didn't go for a walk.

Derin's lips curled into a cruel grin and he said "I am not as foolish as you think. Men, attack!"

Half a dozen men appeared. Four of them wore black armor that looked suspiciously like Kevlar. One of the armored men held a shield over his head that was almost as big as a minivan. Two others carried javelins. The other one carried a great sword as tall as Jack. Another carried ten loaded crossbows in his arms. However, the last person was the thriller.

Thekorion leaned casually on the wall, his face spread in a grin. "Jack, we meet again."

Jack glared at Thekorion in rage. "I'm not surprised. I know evil when I see it."

"Ah, Jack," Thekorion replied. "I believe you have a battle to fight."

Jack preferred a nice sunny day at the park to fighting duels, but he didn't seem to have a choice. He raised his sword, hoping that it wasn't the last thing he did.

The Duel

Count grabbed a cross bow and shot. It flew with deadly accuracy, missing Jack's ear by few centimeters. It shot the glass window, shattering it instantly. The man with the shield guarded two javelin throwers as they charged. The sword man advanced with murder in his eyes. All of this had happened in less than a minute. If this was how they fought, Jack was dead.

* * * * *

"Thekerion's boss is the Emperor of demons, Ruler of sorceress and lord to death. The Evil God."

Katie continued to tell Luke, "Jack was sent just so he could be killed. You have to save him. He could be the start of a good cause. For Jack to do that, he has to be alive. So you have to save him."

Luke needed no more explanation. He took off running.

As Jack ran, another quarrel took flight. The swordsman ran at Jack, recklessly swinging and thrashing. *"Duck"* thought Jack. *"Stab, parry, slash, downwards cut, sidestep."* He was tiring with every blow he blocked, every cut he deflected and every strike he made.

Quarrels flew past him as he sidestepped attacks. The javelin men advanced as the swordsman sparred with Jack.

The swordsman cut downwards and roared.

"He is trying to get me helpless," Jack thought.

"In that case, I'm not hesitating to fight."

"Do you surrender?" The swordsman asked as he made a low cut at Jack's knees. "Answer me!"

Jack ducked away from the cut and answered with a series of fluid, circular cuts.

The swordsman parried and cut forward.

"His elbow was exposed."

Jack lunged forward at the man's elbow. A roar of pain told him that he drove the sword into his elbow.

The swordsman's roar of pain was deafening.

Then, Jack saw the swordsman's sword coming towards his own.

"The swordsman was trying to disarm me."

He realized that at the last second. The sword was coming at him. The swordsman's face was victorious as his sword went into a wide arc at Jack's sword. His victory didn't last long.

Jack had drawn away. He lashed out quickly. With all his strength behind his sword, he impaled the swordsman through his breastplate. The swords man doubled over and then fell into the path of shield carrier. The shield carrier tripped over the swords man and toppled onto him.

"Two down, three more to go."

The last quarrels took flight. It whizzed past Jack and shattered a glass vase. Out of weapons, The Count grabbed a shield from the display and hurled it at Jack with a heave. It missed and hit the javelin man who fell with a groan, spear still in hand. The other one roared a battle cry and charged at Jack. Jack danced away and swatted aside the spear. The man dropped his spear and threw himself to the ground. His hand closed around the fallen swordsman's sword. He got to his feet quickly and charged. His sword sped over Jack in an arc. Jack lashed out and answered with a thrust to the chest. The man stepped away and aimed a thrust at Jack's chest. Jack parried.

It was a grave mistake.

The force of the sword sent him hurtling to the ground. His sword skittered across the floor.

The man leaned over Jack triumphantly.

He looked over at Derin. "May I do the honors, sir?"

Derin nodded. "Since you have finally defeated him, you may do the honors."

The man raised his sword over Jack.

Then, his eyes bulged. His body went rigid and fell. A knife was protruding out of his back. A girl stood behind him, her hand on the knife

Emmera was wearing a sleeveless blue gown with a silver belt studded with aquamarine, pearls and diamonds. Hanging from her ears were drooping pearl earrings, a heavy golden locket shining bright .Her long brown hair was set loose. She wore white gloves and ivory boots. Her smile was radiant. "Hello Jack," she said.

Soldiers in Sight

The Count was tied up.

"We've won," Jack growled. "You're tied up. You'll tell us where the enemy location is, or else..." He let the threat hang in the air.

The Count let out a harsh laugh. "The enemy is in your midst."

Jack gritted his teeth and turned towards Emmera. "I'm afraid he is right."

Emmera looked perplexed. "What do you mean? The enemies are in disguise?"

The Count laughed again. "The enemy needs no disguise."

Jack nodded. "The enemy is... Thekorion."

Emmera's face was grave. "I suspected this for a long time. But I don't get how he could fit into everything."

"I could tell you," The Count said. "It's very surprising. And besides, Thekorion himself could bring down Galobia. I could tell you everything. The only price is that you have to let me go."

Jack looked down at The Count, his eyes hard. "I don't believe you," he said. "Come on, Emmera. Let's go."

He turned to leave.

As soon as Jack and Emmera were out of sight, a boy slipped into the room and undid the knots. "There is an enemy far north," he said.

Jack and Emmera dashed out the front door before anybody could serve them breakfast, although Jack wouldn't turn down any. Obviously.

Luke dashed. Part of him knew that was crazy, but his body did not listen to that part whatsoever. He ran for one cause. *"Get to Jack. Warn him before it's too late..."*

Jack and Emmera settled themselves in the heart of the forest. "So," Jack said. "Why are you dressed like a princess?"

"Well," Emmera said. "I was supposed to be a princess, so I had to play up the part. I went to a salon, and got my hair done. Then, I bought a dress."

"There's a salon here?" Jack asked. "And how do you know where it is?"

Emmera gave a wry smile. "I know a thing or two."

"Well, I still don't get how you got to me at the right time."

Emera shrugged. "I could give you a long speech on how lucky I am and getting to the right place at the right time, but to be honest, I didn't think that I could really be helping you in any way if I spent time in a salon, getting my hair done. Really, I think that getting your hair done and getting dresses are for girly girls."

"Me too," Jack said. "But then again, I'm not a girl.

"Obviously. You would make a weird girl. Most girls aren't that temperamental. "

"I wish people wouldn't call me that."

"Some things, you have to endure," Emmera said.

She settled back on the grass. "I'll take the first shift. You sleep."

Jack closed his eyes and fell asleep.

When he woke up, the first thing he heard was Emmera's voice. "Soldiers in sight! Run!"

Jack sat up, all traces of drowsiness gone.

"Soldiers? Whe-"

"There." Emmera pointed franticly to the Inn. "Soldiers from the Inn. They don't seem happy that we tied up Derin."

Emmera had her travel clothes on, her backpack slung over her shoulder. All signs of beauty were replaced by the weight of panic.

Jack stood up and grabbed his backpack. He slung it over his shoulder and stood up. "Let's go."

Escape Times Two

Luke ran without any supplies, he tried to get to Jack. As soon as he had gotten through the gates, soldiers were on his tail. If they caught him he would almost definitely be dead. He ran for his life.

A mile away Jack and Emmera were doing the same. They had a whole crowd on their tail. It included a few cavalry members, half a dozen swords men, and a whole frenzy of town folks who had decided to join the chase. This was bad, very bad.

As the soldiers closed in around Luke, they held weapons in a threatening way and screwed their faces in a look that said, *"Give up and maybe I will spare you. Run and we'll catch you. But if you think you can escape............."*

Luke was getting tired and more importantly scared. He stopped suddenly when one of the men was a foot away from him. An arrow had hit him square into the chest. Groaning, he fell.

Luke skidded to a stop, confused and confounded. At that moment, four arrows went flying. More soldiers went down. Faces emerged from all four trees. More archers were perched on them, patient as they set the trap.

Then, at that moment, chaos broke out. Arrows took flight. More soldiers went down, groaning. A look of surprise was frozen on each of their faces as they fell. Luke was about to sigh in relief, but a new thought occurred to him. Luke thought *"What if the archers target was me?"* One of the archers raised his bow, put the arrow to the string and raised it to Luke's heart. *"Yes,"* the archers face said. *"We want you."*

The archer shifted on his tree and faced Luke. "Hey, you " he yelled. "It is time we take you to Varalon ". He broke off when a galloping horse came into view. A cloaked rider sat atop it, hand on its neck. The figure jumped off and raised his hand in a salute to the archer. "So, we meet again. I see that you have stooped down to capturing children." He turned to Luke. "If I were you boy, I would jump on the horse and let me take you for a ride."

"It's not your spot to take him anywhere Adraverkee, "the archer growled. He then leaped from the tree and ambled over to Adraverkee. "Take him and my archers shall pierce you through the heart."

"Go ahead" the cloaked figure Adraverkee shot back. "Let us see if your men are weaker than you."

"They are not fooling around," the archer warned. "Your arrogance will die with you."

They came to a face off, looking like two kids arguing about sports teams, except much more serious. One could end up dead. Suddenly, arguing about sports teams seemed like it was immature.

Adraverkee stood three inches fuller but the archer didn't look any less intimidating. After a minute, the archer broke face contact and stepped back. He looked to his archers and nodded.

Almost immediately three arrows took flight. Adraverkee dropped down and rolled. The archer tried to intercept but instead of blocking Adraverkee, he tripped over him and landed with one of his own men's arrows was about to strike. He rolled out of the range quickly and yelled at his men to get down.

They climbed down awkwardly until a throwing star had sprouted from their chest. In a quick and fluid motion, Adraverkee had thrown three stars.

The archers fell, motionless.

The remaining archers tried to back up, but before anybody could go back one inch, a sword was at his throat. "There is nobody to help you now," Adraverkee growled his eyes boring into soldiers, "I just wish I had a card that celebrates death day. You will be heading one soon."

At that second, the archer fell, a spear striking through his heart. "We have company." Adverkee growled. He was right.

Jack and Emmera were quickly overtaken, the swords men came in, brandishing swords crazily, as if they had not got a single minute of training. The cavalry warriors, however, were more organized. They made a circle around the swords men, Jack, and Emmera.

The town people had a gathered around and were looking at the soldiers and smiling as if they expected a spectacle. Some were yelling at the soldiers to beat the kids up , while others were placing bets on how easily the soldier's would win. Money was being exchanged. Women gossiped and kids chatted. In short, they were having a great time. Jack and Emmera obviously were not having a good time. They wouldn't be in one piece by the time it ended. This spectacle sounded like fun, lots of fun.

World War III

An armored man emerged from behind the trees. His chest gleamed with badges, his belt carried multiple knives, and his chain mail armor was rusted and dented badly from battle. His head was covered with a Spartan's helmet. Only his eyes were visible. All they carried were hate.

He held a sword in his right hand.

"The Count," Adraverkee growled. He pushed Luke back. "Don't run."

"*If I ran,*" Luke thought, *"I would just be digging up my own grave."*

A horn sounded in the distance. The Spectacle had begun.

The crowd grew excited. All of their faces turned from each other to the "stage". The air was filled with noises. The audience had wide smiles on their faces. Some were even spreading blankets on the ground and sitting down like they were having a picnic. They all pulled bread or fruit from small pouches, but the air of entertainment was even more appealing to their taste.

Adraverkee and The Count stood inches from each other. The Count had drawn his sword, and Adraverkee had armed himself with another throwing star. They stood there silent, for at least a minute, until The Count broke silence. "Give up," he simply said. "Or else ….."

"Or else what," Adraverkee challenged "You kill yourself?"

"My," a voice said behind them. "I thought my guests would have the manners to let me kill them." A man stepped into view and bowed. It was Varolon.

The horn sounded again. This time, everyone went quite. All the chatter died. All the munching stopped. Everyone sat and didn't move, hushed. The soldiers stopped sharpening their weapons and stood to attention.

Another time, the horn sounded. At that moment, a man from the crowd stood. He was an old man with a grey beard that flowed down to his chest. His skin was wrinkled and bruised. He wore loose grey robes over a tunic, his feet bare.

"Ladies and Gentleman," he began. "Residents of the One Inn, we are punishing the vagabonds who disturbed our peace. We will of course, dispose of them entertainingly. You, obviously, will have to pay to watch this spectacle. Nourishing food, clothing to keep us warm and…" He paused for a moment. "And of course money!!! In return you will get what we promise. Pure entertainment."

The crowd went wild. They tossed bags of money onto the stadium.

"Yes, that's the spirit." The man roared. "That's-"

His words were cut short when a small man on horseback raced towards "the stadium." "Quick" he yelled his voice hoarse. "Shah Addure is coming."

Luke shuddered at the sight of the man. His skin was tan and wrinkled, without any hair on his face. His grey eyes were narrow and bloodshot. His lips were a faint brown line across his face. His chin was square. His face was covered with bruises and ugly scars from battle. But this time, the only people who were going to get bruised were the people opposing him. "I want the boy. Give him to me."

The crowd panicked as a small group of horseback riders came into view. The air was filled with both the distance sound of horses and buzz of the frightened townspeople. The old man who had been giving the speech was now shouting for order. His voice however, was drained by the frightened crowd. Many people were trying to talk their way through the crowd, but soon, they changed their tactics to old-fashioned shoving. The few stragglers who were trying to stay and listen to the old man were only hoping that he could get them out safely. The messenger who had reported the attack, however, was only spreading the haze of panic.

"Go," he yelled. "Save yourself!" The old man had called the soldiers to block the exit, but they weren't listening. They were running with the crowd, hoping for no casualties.

One of them, remembering Jack and Emmera, grabbed them by the scruffs of their necks before they could be swept into the crowd. "Not going to escape now," he growled. He lifted them off the ground and ran as the horsemen closed in. Among the horsemen was a chariot and in it was Shah Addure himself.

The tall man was dressed in a golden armor that caught light of the sun. He was standing, shouting orders to his men. The men rode on black horses, wore black leather armor, and carried black weapons.

As they closed in, the people changed their minds. They drew back, and let the soldiers fight. The five swordsmen drew small, homemade matches from their pockets. The three cavalry members hastily readied their weapons. Their power looked pathetic next to the enemy. The soldier carrying Jack and Emmera dropped them and jogged after the rest of the soldiers.

The swordsmen lit their matches, the cavalry riders readied themselves for the charge, and the old man signaled for them to attack.

Demons

As soon as the troops met in combat, the old man's swordsmen flung there matches into the demon ranks. Flames spread through the demons, and the whole army burst into flames.

"Yes", the old man yelled. "We have done it!"

"Oh, I don't think so," A voice growled from inside the fire. "This is just a beginning."

The smoke and fire rose. That's when he appeared. Shah Addure became visible in the center. The armor had not been burned, but his attitude was flamed. "Fools!" He yelled.

"You haven't even met my army."

"Men," Varolon roared. "Attack them".

A dozen armed men walked out from behind the shadows. They were all armed with a sword, spear, bow, and an assortment of knifes. "I suggest you yield," Varolon said, pressing a sword into The Count's throat. "Or you will soon be dead."

The flames died and Addure stepped out of them. "I am not done yet," he yelled. "My real army approaches." He pointed to the west. A large army was approaching with surprising speed. A mix of archers, cavalry, foot soldiers and battering rams. There were even some stampeding elephants in the group.

"See," he boomed. "I don't only rain on a parade. I storm on it!"

"I don't think so," the old man returned confidently.

All the attention was drawn to him.

"Look," he pointed towards the south as conch horn blew in the distance. "The rebels are coming"

Thekorion gazed down at the bustling city. It was loud, yet peaceful. But if his plan succeeded, the place would be in ruins. He just needed a person who would help him. With that person in reach, Thekorion wouldn't let go. He needed Jared Revohk.

The rebels advanced with aggression. Many rode on horseback. Others ran. Archers rode on chariots with their bows drawn. The knights had their lances ready, and the foot soldiers carried harpoons. Others brandished maces, swords, daggers, shields, and axes.

The whole army moved in a diamond formation. The outmost layer was made of locked shields in harpoons. Knights made up the next line, their weapons drawn. The final layer was made of archers.

"Well, Well," Addure snarled. "I see we have company. Men, attack!"

"Rebels," the old man shouted. "This is your chance to win!"

They shot forward, yelling in defiance. The weapons raised, they met the charge.

As the armies met, their forces spread out. Knights threw their spears and drew swords. Shield carriers scattered. Archers fired their arrows. Foot soldiers started to brandish their weapons. Skirmishes broke out. Weapons met shields. Legions of arrows took flight. Weapons began to clash furiously.

The rebel army scattered. They drew back and then attack with renewed speed. They met the demon army violently with sweeping motions of their weapons.

Swords gleamed in the sunlight. Spears flew. The rain of arrows was deadly. Swords cut down staffs. Soldiers dropped their broken weapons and charged barehanded. The knights had jumped of their horses and advanced on foot. Soldiers drew back as catapults were launched.

As the battle raged, the crowd of people were swept into the mix of the soldiers. Some were running through the maze of soldiers, while others were taking cover behind the broken chariots.

Jack and Emmera were swept into the battle. Around them, it's raged. Swords met.

Arrows flew through the air. Some found their mark while others fell to the ground, useless.

Soldiers who had lost all other weapons were fighting with daggers. Some enemy soldiers, seeing Jack and Emmera, charged. They went back to back, Jack hacking and slashing until they fell back. Emmera dispatched many soldiers with a borrowed sword, but more soldiers took their place.

Adduare was watching all of this from a distance. He watched as his army slowly over took the rebels. They were being dominated by the relentless attacks of the demon army. The few rebels who remained standing were held back by demons. This battle was over for them.

"It's time to give a victory speech."

Addure signaled for silence but he proceeded without waiting for it. "My winning demon army and the loosing rebels," as soon as this was said, the people's voices died out. "My victory was made by a demon.

But not one soldier from my demon army could receive this position of honor." His eyes drifted to Jack, then continued. "The demon is within our midst. His name is Jack Wridor".

Deception

The first feeling to go through Jack was disbelief. Then anger. Then thoughtfulness, *"would it make sense?"* Jack wondered. *"No,"* he said to himself but deep down, he couldn't argue.

He only had seconds to register this before he was hit by a flying tackle.

Emmera was on him, pummeling him with her fist. Her face was screwed in anger.

"You are an agent of demons," she yelled into his face. "You deserve to be punished!" She slammed her fist onto him.

This was when power surged through him. A single thought was all he needed. *"I need to stop her no matter what."*

His brain went into focus suddenly. He felt a tingling sensation creep into him. It started slowly, but in a few seconds, it felt like electricity was surging through him. *"We had been waiting for you to recognize your power,"* a voice said inside of him.

His arms moved by himself. He blocked Emmera's punches and added one of his own. She toppled.

"I am," he whispered. "I am. **I am!"** He looked up at Addure. "But I will fight you."

His muscles tightened. He let out a battle cry and attacked.

The demons look shocked. But it didn't last long. They drew their weapons, let out battle cries of their own, and charged.

Jack raised his sword and quickly engaged the demons in combat.

He hacked, thrust, and stabbed under their guard. The remaining rebels raised their swords and called a charge.

The rebels clashed furiously with demon army. The remaining rebel archers knocked their arrows and let go.

The demons aimed their attacks on Jack. As they attacked, Jack applied attacks of his own. He brought his sword down on demons, cutting them down minute after minute. The demons hammered him with their swords, only to be deflected. Jack blocked attacks from all different attacks, his swords spinning and his hand moving automatically.

He cut down demon by demon, dispatching them quickly.

Rage boiled inside of him. A rage, that didn't belong to him. For now, he wasn't a human. He was a pillar of rage.

He hacked through ranks. Every demon in sight of him ran. The rebels gathered in small squads and attacked. The battle was on.

"To me!" The old man yelled. "To me!" The rebels gathered around him, a few straggling numbers against the huge demon army. "Archers, grab your final arrows. Hit weak spots. No sense wasting arrows." The archers knocked their arrows and let them go.

The legion of arrows took flight. Many demons fell, groaning.

"Soldiers, advance," the old man shouted. The rebels drew swords and charged. "The demons will conquer," A demon soldier snarled as he parried a rebel strike. "Look."

A new regiment marched into the battlefield.

They weren't rebels.

The new regiment swooped down with their weapons drawn. Archers knocked their arrows and let them fly. The rebels went down.

The old man was caught up in a melee in the middle of the action. He swirled, slashed, stabbed and hacked. The old man was hopelessly out numbered, no matter how he fought. His men had fallen, and the demons were getting stronger. Jack knew that the battle was over. He turned around and fled.

When Emmera woke up she was in a wagon. It was crowded with many other people, huddled to gather against the sand browsing into the wagon. She knew what this meant. She had been captured by the enemy.

Jack stopped, trying to catch his breath. Sand was swirling around him, blowing into his eyes. *"Soon there will be a sandstorm,"* Jack thought grimly. He had to get out of there, or soon he will be buried in sand ....

The door opened, and Jared Revohk stepped in. He shunted into the room and helped himself to a chair. "Really, Thek," Jared said. "What do you need me to do now? Rob a Bank? Set Galobia on fire? Attack the Capital?" His voice was dripping with sarcasm.

"Well, as for attacking the Capital," Thekarion said warily," you'll have to do that eventually. But, the good news is, eventually might not be that long anymore. Little

Emmera has been captured, and we've arranged for Jack to be killed"

"Never," Count Derin countered, ignoring the sword point at his throat. "I don't fear you".

"What did you say?"Varolon growled, digging the sword point further.

"I don't fear you," Count Derin said." I won't yield.

Varalon looked at his guards. "Leave them," he yelled. He dropped his sword to the ground. "Capture Derin." Then he turned, and stepped into the shadows.

Jared's face spread into a leer. "Great" he said. "We can join forces with the Great Sorcerer very soon now."

"Weeell," Thekerion said," L.J. came back to the city. He's the only problem. If you, uh, get rid of him tonight, we can steam ahead. Then, we will join forces with the Great Sorcerer."

Jared nodded." I will get rid of him. I'll prove my worth to The Great Sorcerer. Not only him, though. I'll prove my worth to Shah Addare. And soon, I'll be proving my worth to the Evil God."

Jared stood in a dark alley, his face shadowed by the nearby buildings. The night was dark and moonless. He had his sword drawn. He just hoped he could get to L.J's building before it was too late.

He crept through the dark streets. There were no street lamps and no people outside. The cobble stone streets were empty. *Good,* Jared thought. *I can make a clean escape.*

Jack collapsed into the sand, and then everything backed out.

The Game

Jack woke up to the sound of cheering crowds. The sound was deafening. There were hundreds of people watching him intently. Nobody looked at each other. Their attention was on the stage. This was Jack's show.

Jared opened the cabin's door quietly and peered inside. He spotted L.J. lying on his bed, asleep.

Jared sauntered into the room and raised his sword over L.J.

"JARED!"

Jared turned with his sword raised. Then he saw the exact thing that he feared.

Standing behind him was Thekorion, flanked by two guards.

"Caught in the act. Trying to kill L.J., one of our best scouts."

He looked at his guards. "What are you waiting for? Seize him."

The guards grabbed Jared roughly and led him.

"The job is done," Thekorion thought. *"Shah Addares plan is working out."*

Jack scanned the field, uncertain of what to do. The crowds cheering grew louder

"The champion has waked at last," a voice said from above him.

Jack looked up. A man stood over him, sword in hand.

"What!" Jack sputtered. "What are you talking about? I'm not a champion."

"Oh, but you are the champion," the man said. "You collapsed in our land, and therefore, you have to play our games. You have no choice."

Jack looked up. "What are the rules?"

The man looked down at Jack. "You will rise. Then, I tell you the rules."

"I'm tired," Jack complained. "It won't be fair if I'm tired."

The man's eyes were hard. "It doesn't matter if you're tired. The game is not a physical game, and therefore, you will be seated. "

Jack stood unsteadily. "What's the game? Explain it."

"Oh," the man said. "I wouldn't call this a game. If you win, you will go free. If you lose, you will be our slave."

"Oh," Jack said. "This sounds fun. I have to play a game where I have to win to get free?"

"Yes," the man answered. "The game is called Kojan. There are many pieces, such as king and queen. I believe you people of earth call it chess.

Jack nodded. At this point, nothing could surprise him. "What if we stale mate? "Then," the man said, "We fight to the death."

"Oh."

"So, shall we start?"

Jack nodded. This was looking worse every minute.

The man snapped. A small kid scuttled towards Jack and set up a chess board in front of him. Then, he scuttled away.

The man looked at Jack. "Will you be playing white, or black?"

Jack shrugged. "Black, I guess."

The man's face held a shadow of a smile. "Very well, then. Let the games begin."

Less than an hour later, the man's voice rang out. "The champion has lost. He is our slave now. Or should I say, Shah Addares slave."

Thekorion stood outside, Shah Addare at his side.

"I have done as you said," Thekorion said. "Now, may I be so bold to ask why you have made me throw Jared into jail."

Shah Addare turned to face Thekorion. "We want Jared to produce as much violence as possible. If you throw Jared into jail, his rage will grow. More rage means more violence."

The guards grabbed Derin roughly. "Wait," he called. He turned towards the guards. "Don't I get a few last words to my friends?"

The guards shifted uncomfortably. Then, they nodded. "You may, but if you try to escape, I swear..."

Derin turned towards Adraverkee. "I'll be back, and when I am back, I'll be back as an ally."

A New Army

Elsewhere, the army of magicians, Wizards and sorcerers was gathering. The Wizards held their Wands, the magicians readied their stuff. All were looking to the north where a new army marched towards them, their faces grim.

All except for the great sorcerer ....

www.ingramcontent.com/pod-product-compliance
Lightning Source LLC
Chambersburg PA
CBHW020557030426
42337CB00013B/1119